His Infernal
Majesty
the Devil

The Luck of the Devil

by

David Damant

49Knights
Independent Publishing House
Edinburgh & Cambridge

ISBN: 978-0-9931975-5-0

Please see page 6 for further copyright information.

The Luck of the Devil

First printing of the first edition

The Luck of the Devil by David Damant

Foreword by Jamie Hayes

Text edited by Dan Lentell

Cover layout and incidental artwork by Carys Boughton

Original portrait of the author by Rupert Shrive

Typesetting by John Tiratsoo

Further information about plays, licensing, current productions and tours can be found at **www.49Knights.com**.

Ingrid, the Baron's Secretary

COPYRIGHT INFORMATION

(See also page 4)

VIDEO-RECORDING OF
AMATEUR PRODUCTIONS

Please note that the copyright laws governing video-recording are extremely complex and that it should not be assumed that any play may be video-recorded for whatever purpose without first obtaining the permission of the appropriate agents. The fact that these plays are published by 49Knights, Independent Publishing House, Edinburgh & Cambridge, does not indicate that video rights are available or that 49Knights controls such rights.

The Baron Sergei Pnetzenny

FOREWORD

The author of this play, David Damant, is a very good friend who knows about the professional arena of world money matters and possesses a fascination for European history. Added to these is a love of the highly melodramatic world of opera. That he had written a mephistophelean melodrama based upon the incipient fall of the Creditanstalt of Vienna during the last century came as no surprise!

They do say "write about what you know," but let's put the devil to one side for now; just so we might remain friends. Both being keen members of The Garrick Club in London, a world famous meeting place for those who adore actors and theatre, that seemed a good a place as any to try it out.

David had rather become our unofficial Club dramaturge and my initial introduction to this popular Club was to direct a series of private performances at his request of opera events, featuring some of the finest voices around and dramatically produced with costumes, lights, smoke and mirrors! An unforgettable evening of the darkest scenes from Mozart's *Don Giovanni*; graveyard and supper scene included, naturally. One abiding memory will be of the Don feeding oysters to two virtually naked ladies.This production returned at a later date due to popular demand.

The Devil is always in the detail and David has a keen eye by which he continually seeks dramatic ingenuity, aligned with innovative theatricality. Given that now the play was <u>his</u> thing it was a delight to come on board as director once again and work with him closely in the preparation of a performance at the Garrick.

We took the large and impressive Morning Room within our Club in which to perform. This contained many fine theatrical portraits and the general grandiose architecture which the room possessed naturally embraced our dramatic ambition of a stately Viennese banking house. The set design, a simple line of raised rostra with an appropriate mahogany desk dressed accordingly at one end, was set 'in traverse'. This allows the audience to be seated either side of the action; thus facing each other. This format is also sometimes referred to as a 'corridor stage'.

Incidentally and in hindsight, I would happily venture to suggest that a staging *in the round* might also be as, if not more, theatrically advantageous for this work, as the closeness of the audience might just be the key to its success. As the dramatic situation only requires the single banking parlour (in practice his office) of one Baron Bretzenny, all you need is this obligatory desk and a phone which makes the staging kindly economic.

There is an intercom desk device by which the Baron receives various phone calls and secretarial messages and can be achieved in various ways. We simply employed a buzzer intercom sound effect with various 'voices off', amplified and containing suitable 'telephone waffle' effect, for those who call in. One actor 'off' with the required voice skills can cover all the masculine phone calls which arrive, likewise the lead actress can double as the 'off stage' secretary to the Baron.

Our casting was impressive, using well-known actors who are also members of the Club, though the casting of the Devil himself came from outside this comfort zone. I had recently been impressed by the performance of Ian Kelly as George III in the West End play *Mr. Foote's Other Leg* playing at the Theatre Royal, Haymarket of which he was also the author. He happily accepted to take the part and was a joy to work with and a very good master of the dark arts required. A fine portrait of the eponymous Samuel Foote, the 18th Century actor, hung upon the wall in our Morning Room; adding a symbiotic touch.

The play is short enough to run without a break and might (just so you know) also be suited to a radio presentation, as the machinations within the sombre and claustrophobic world of Viennese banking seems to draw in and capture the attention of the listener in a particular way.

The Garrick Club was always going to produce an informative and attentive audience. Seeing a certain acclaimed actor, one much admired for his classic portrayal of a character abundantly possessed of ze little grey cells, taking his seat in the front row rather confirmed this! The arresting narrative of the work unfolds over a series of scenes (the timescale of which takes in two days of a banking crash) and we incorporated live piano music (Viennese waltzes, of course) to create the suitable atmosphere for these natural breaks.

The whole event was rehearsed in a single day, billed simply as *a rehearsed reading* and this is clearly achievable with an experienced group of actors. The play was very warmly received. I guess the Devil always gets the best lines, but the rest that are spoken seemed to produce an intriguing theatrical mix.

I wish this piece a productive future in any future incantations; wherever they may occur.

- Jamie Hayes, January 2017
Director of *The Luck of the Devil*

Schmidt, the Baron's Clerk

INTRODUCTION

When the New York stock market crashed in October 1929 there followed a financial and then an economic panic throughout the world. In Europe the crucial event, which tipped everything into a deep depression, was the failure, in May 1931, of the great Austrian bank, the Creditanstalt. Anyone running a bank in the run up to that event, like the Baron Bretzenny of this play, was faced with impossible financial odds.

Impossible, unless money could be raised from some new, unearthly source.

The myth of the Devil offering desirable things to humans in exchange for their souls is long lived. Sometimes youth and beauty are offered in place of material gain. Among the largess bestowed on Marlowe's Faust is the ability to provide the Duchess Vanholt with a dish of ripe grapes in "the dead time of the winter" - a supernatural feat achieved today by a trip to Tescos. In the case of Baron Bretzenny the temptation is money.

The literary variations on this theme have been numerous. Sometimes, for example, the human being tries to get the soul back. In what follows, when the Devil does his deal with the Baron the evolution of events is a tad more complex. Still, we should be warned that, more usually, "he who sups with the Devil needs a very long spoon."

The concept of a Devil is not an arbitrary fiction. As the psychiatrist Carl Jung said, if the Christian religion is not true, it must be psychologically valid, since otherwise it would not have succeeded. The Devil reflects a part of our human psyche which may be imaginary and even, as in this play, humorously treated - but it is not all myth.

The writing of this play came to me one morning at 6 am. I had finished the first draft before (a latish) breakfast. For some time I had been revolving, semi-consciously, the idea of the Devil being thwarted by the Church, and having to ask for human assistance. The play just wrote itself onto the computer, and only some polishing was necessary later, plus some elaboration of the part played in the drama by Madame Bernhardi.

It can be argued that aristocratic titles were abolished in Austria in 1918, that the currency was not Crowns, and that bank transfers were not in 1931 as rapid as they are now. But I have written a play, not a documentary.

- David Damant
January 2017

The Luck of the Devil

First performed in the Morning Room of the Garrick Club, London, on Monday 1st February 2016.

Written by David Damant

Performed by

Roger Braban
The Baron Sergei Bretzenny
Sophie Louise-Dann
Ingrid as well as Madame Astrid Bernhardi
Stephen Thorne
Schultmann, Count Eisenthal, and also Schmidt
Andrew Hammond
His Eminence the Cardinal Archbishop of Vienna
George Layton
Monsignor Valence

and
Ian Kelly
His Infernal Majesty the Devil

Piano accompaniment by Jean Rigby

Directed and designed by Jamie Hayes

Sound technician Graham Richards

The play lasts approximately 75 mins including piano intervals

★ ★ ★ ★ ★

All profits from this publication will be contributed to the Garrick Charitable Trust, details of which can be found in the "About the Garrick Club" section of the Garrick Club website.

Note on the text: SFX = sound effect; FX = lighting/pyrotechnical effect; SR = stage right; SL = stage left; SC = stage centre.

CHARACTERS IN ORDER OF APPEARANCE

Ingrid
the Baron's Secretary

The Baron Sergei Bretzenny
titular owner of a small, aristocratic, but troubled, Viennese banking house

Schultmann
the Baron's close friend

Schmidt
the Baron's clerk

His Infernal Majesty the Devil

Madame Astrid Bernhardi
the Baron's lover

Monsignor Valence
a priest attached to the Cardinal's office

His Eminence the Cardinal Archbishop of Vienna

Count Eisenthal
the Austrian Minister of Finance

ACTS

The play is set in Vienna during the terrible economic depression which followed the Wall Street crash of 1929, and shortly before the collapse of the great Austrian bank the Creditanstalt in May 1931.

Act 1 - The scene is set in the Banking Parlour of the Bank Bretzenny
Act 2 - The same, that afternoon
Act 3 - The same, the next morning

The original production was a rehearsed reading performed in the Morning Room of the Garrick Club, London. The set design, a simple line of raised rostra, featured a mahogany desk, dressed accordingly, at one end. Traverse seating allowed the audience to be seated either side of the action.

A buzzer intercom SFX announced the "entry" of those characters who did not appear in the Baron's office, but who were rather imagined to be heard through the telecom / telephone. The voices of actors Sophie Louise-Dann (in the role of Ingrid) and Stephen Thorne (as Schultmann, Schmidt, and Count Eisenthal), the voices off, were instead amplified along with a suitable telephone waffle SFX.

Madame
Bernhardi

ACT 1

[*Morning. BARON is sitting at his desk making calculations on various slips of paper with a pencil. He displays a rigid calm. SFX intercom.*]

INGRID:	Herr Baron, the Cardinal's office asks if they can send someone round to collect the 100 Crowns you have subscribed to the Cardinal's fund.
BARON:	Of course, yes; I hope they don't send that garrulous Monsignor Valence who can't stop talking!
INGRID:	The Cardinal's secretary tells me that the Monsignor 's heart is in the right place, sir.
BARON:	Well Ingrid I wish his tongue was also in the right place, which is behind a gag. Anyway, arrange it.
INGRID:	Very good, sir.
BARON:	Well with what I have in the safe I can just about manage a hundred. And then CAPUT! Nothing except the useful reserve I have for disappearing to Sicily. No one will find me there.

[*Looks at the calculations he has been working on.*]

Minus 1,625,000 Crowns. Quite a deficit. And as far as I can see I have disguised the matter - no one suspects I am bust.....for the moment anyway.....not bad, Bretzenny.

[*SFX intercom.*]

INGRID: Herr Schultmann is on the phone sir.

BARON: Oh good, thank you. [*Speaks into the telephone.*] Morning Schultmann.

SCHULTMANN: Morning old boy.....I was at the Exchange earlier and there were rumours in the market that you were in difficulties.

BARON: They should be worrying about the Creditanstalt.

SCHULTMANN: Well I didn't say that as I don't believe in encouraging the rumour mill but I did say that people shouldn't go round just repeating gossip.

BARON: Well thank you. But it is all very wearing.

SCHULTMANN: Anyway old boy are you lunching at the Club today?

BARON: No. [*He hesitates slightly.*] I have another appointment.

SCHULTMANN: Pity as Grossmann will be there. He is raising money for that pavilion at the Race Course.

BARON: Yes I heard of his gilded cage and I am glad not to meet him. Anyway with the financial world being in turmoil after the Wall Street crash why is he pursuing an extravagant idea like that?

SCHULTMANN: He thinks it will raise confidence.

BARON: I would guarantee it's just vanity on his
                   part.

SCHULTMANN: I thought that if you met him at the Club
                   you could question him informally as it
                   were.

BARON: No thank you. And I cannot stand his
                   lectures on atheism. He just goes on and
                   on about the non existence of God.

SCHULTMANN: You're an atheist yourself.

BARON: Yes but I don't bore the pants off people by
                   preaching about it.

SCHULTMANN: Yes you are more sensible. But you are the
                   number two atheist in Vienna!

BARON: No doubt. But I have to go... Have a good
                   lunch.

SCHULTMANN: OK, OK old boy I will let you get on.

[SFX *intercom*.]

INGRID: The office sir.[1]

BARON: Please put him through. [*Speaks into the
                   telephone.*] Bretzenny.

SCHMIDT: [*Worried.*] Good morning Herr Baron.

---

1 In a grand bank of the period the rooms in which the owners / partners would sit
to make decisions, or consult with eminent clients, would be referred to as a banking
parlour. The reference here is to the office, to that administrative part of the bank,
where records would kept, where clerks would clerk, and so on. These functions
would be housed in another part of the building or in unconnected premises round
the corner from the more intimate, sophisticated banking parlour. - DD

BARON: Good morning Schmidt.

SCHMIDT: Sir, the transfers have not arrived.

BARON: Really that is boring. I gave very clear instructions. Where are we as regards our payments?

SCHMIDT: There are only the payments which I have already listed for you as overdue, sir, and I added of course the 93,000 for the Creditanstalt next week.

BARON: Fine - I will chase the transfers.

SCHMIDT: [*His voice grows urgent.*] And Herr Baron we have to send the official return to the Ministry of Finance today.

BARON: I have that in mind. Keep me informed of any developments.

SCHMIDT: Yes indeed Sir.

[*BARON puts down telephone rather deliberately.*]

BARON: Well that's the end of the road I think.

[*Pause.*]

                    So my little reserve for the disappearance to Italy will soon be needed.

[*Puts head in hands.*]

[*THE DEVIL appears. He is tall and immaculately dressed in a dark morning coat. Bretzenny tries the intercom and the phone but they do not respond.*]

THE DEVIL: I regret that I have cut both lines.

[*BARON rises.*]

                        And the door will not open.

BARON: Who the devil are you?

THE DEVIL: Well expressed. I AM the Devil.

BARON: You are clearly mad.

[*Feels in drawer for pistol.*]

THE DEVIL: You keep a pistol in the drawer as a
                        precaution against intruders but it is not
                        loaded. It is no use without bullets...

[*BARON freezes.*]

                        ...And anyway I am immortal. You could
                        fire at me as much as you like and I would
                        not be affected. Though I suppose the
                        bullets would spoil my morning coat.

[*THE DEVIL strokes his morning coat, rather vainly. Bretzenny pauses and
then recollects himself and sits down.*]

BARON: Please sit down. I can give you five minutes.
                        What are you after?

[*THE DEVIL sits.*]

THE DEVIL: Your soul of course. Why else does
                        the Devil visit a human? I have wide
                        responsibilities in the world, but always
                        time for the capture of souls.

BARON: I have no soul. All that is a primitive myth.

THE DEVIL: Then you will have no difficulty in exchanging it.

BARON: For what?

THE DEVIL: 1,625,000 Crowns. [*BARON reacts to this exact figure.*] But I think you need a bit extra in view of today's report to the Ministry of Finance. Say 1,925,000 Crowns. In exchange for your non-existent soul. That will mean you can send the return to the Ministry with a balance of 297,000 Crowns. A very tidy sum to send in.

BARON: [*Cynically.*] I suppose you want me to sign the agreement in my blood.

THE DEVIL: Oh no. That is just a dramatic fiction you humans have invented. Quite amusing. I know we have settled the deal even though you think you have no soul. But as I know that you have a soul I am perfectly satisfied and I will put matters in train later today. The other human I saw this morning was not so sensible.

BARON: And who was that?

THE DEVIL: You will appreciate that I extend to everyone the discretion I promise to you.

BARON: At least in this way you act like a gentleman.

THE DEVIL: I hope you do not suggest that the Devil is not a gentleman? I may not be popular but I am always discreet. [*Rises.*] And I hope polite. [*Bows slightly.*] But now I must return to my manifold duties in the propagation of Evil. Good morning.

[*THE DEVIL exits. After a moment to gain control of himself, BARON activates the intercom.*]

BARON: Ingrid - who was the gentleman who has just left my office?

INGRID: There was no one sir. No one has been here since the morning letters came earlier.

BARON: I see. Thank you. [*Thinks quickly.*] Yes of course he used the other door.

[*Pause. BARON wipes his hand across his brow.*]

[*SFX intercom.*]

INGRID: Madame Bernhardi is here, Herr Baron.

[*BARON looks very concerned but then decides to handle the matter conventionally.*]

BARON: Please show her in.

[*He stands up and looks rather menacing. Madame Bernhardi enters. She is very elegantly dressed but with an almost unnoticeable touch of over smartness.*]

BARON: I asked you never to call here.

MME BERNHARDI: I know, and I never have and never will again but...

BARON: Sit down and explain yourself.

[*He sits. She sits.*]

MME BERNHARDI: Sergei...

BARON: It is better to call me Baron in the office.

MME BERNHARDI: Yes. Sergei, Herr Grossmann threatens to reveal the truth about my son, Peter.

BARON: Is Grossmann one of your... friends?

MME BERNHARDI: No. I do not care for him at all.

BARON: And why should he wish to tell anyone about your youthful indiscretion?

MME BERNHARDI: He will do so unless I submit to his... to him.

BARON: The man is a cad.

MME BERNHARDI: That does not help me.

BARON: How long has this been going on?

MME BERNHARDI: He has been a nuisance for a long time. The threat - only a week - but I need a solution soon. You know my position in Viennese society. I am invited, but only just. I would be destroyed if it appeared that I had a son out of wedlock.

BARON: Let me think about this Astrid. Perhaps some of your... lovers could help.

MME BERNHARDI: It is unkind of you to put it like that.

BARON: I am sorry my dear, but it something to consider... It Peter doing well? Is an English public school suiting him?

MME BERNHARDI: Oh yes. [*She brightens up.*] He is so successful. He is one of the Eton pair in the Public Schools racquets competition. And being able to keep him at Eton justifies my lifestyle, so that I can afford the fees.

BARON: Well... Let us meet in the next day or two. But somewhere else, not here.

MME BERNHARDI: Yes of course... but I needed to explain...

BARON: I understand. [*More fondly.*] For now, au revoir. And I will give all my attention to finding a solution. After so many years together...

MME BERNHARDI: Yes my dear. You know that you are more to me than just a lover.

BARON: On my side also. And now good morning Madame.

MME BERNHARDI: Good morning, Baron.

BARON: [*Into the intercom.*] Ingrid – please show Madame Bernhardi out.

[*MME BERNHARDI exits.*]

BARON: I suppose that fifty years ago I would have challenged Grossmann to a duel. It would have to be pistols. No one can beat him with a rapier or sabre.

[*SFX intercom.*]

INGRID:	The office sir.
BARON:	Put him though. [*Very crossly.*] Yes Schmidt.
SCHMIDT:	[*Rather excited.*] Sir we have received 1,925,000 Crowns.
BARON:	All together? [*Inventing words as he goes along.*] I thought there would be separate transfers. What was the source in this case?
SCHMIDT:	That's not clear sir. It is very strange.
BARON:	[*Sharply.*] It is not at all strange Schmidt.
SCHMIDT:	Oh, sorry sir, but I was puzzled.
BARON:	Well don't be. Complete all the necessary transactions and send me a note of the balance.
SCHMIDT:	Yes sir. And shall I also clear some routine payments that have accumulated?
BARON:	Yes. And put the amount for the Creditanstalt out overnight till it is due.
SCHMIDT:	Yes sir. I will send you a reconciliation, and complete the return to the Ministry of Finance.
BARON:	Good - and telephone me the balance before sending the return.
SCHMIDT:	Yes sir. Incidentally I have heard from a clerk that the Minister of Finance himself

is looking at every one of the returns from the banks, immediately they come in.

BARON: That would not be surprising in present circumstances.

SCHMIDT: No sir. Thank you, sir.

[*BARON puts down telephone. SFX intercom.*]

INGRID: Herr Baron, Monsignor Valence from the Cardinal's office is here.

BARON: Show him in.

[*BARON rises. Enter a Monsignor VALENCE, a very neatly dressed and garrulous priest.*]

VALENCE: My dear Baron, we are so pleased to have a contribution to the Cardinal's fund from such a distinguished bank. The Cardinal is delighted and I am sure that...

BARON: I am pleased to contribute Monsignor. I will write a cheque.

[*BARON sits. He takes out cheque book and pen and writes.*]

VALENCE: At the Cardinal's office we were saying only yesterday that the support of so many members of the financial world is so gratifying, especially at this confused time. We hope that despite the circumstances we shall be able to announce the success of his appeal in a week or two, or at any rate in a month.

It will be announced in the newspapers.
Many of the editors have expressed interest
in the fund and we are hoping that they
will give us a very good coverage. And of
course the Cardinal is very pleased with
the response we have seen.

Even the former Imperial and Royal house
has most generously sent a contribution
from abroad, though the amount of course
remains private. I think we can be very
satisfied...

[*BARON hands the cheque to VALENCE.*]

Oh thank you.

VALENCE: But my dear Baron - we had you entered for
                100 Crowns and this is for 1,000.

BARON: I believe the Cardinal's fund is certainly a
                very worthy cause.

VALENCE: His Eminence will be delighted. Oh! and
                I can inform him now as he is conducting
                Mass at St Michael's just across the road.
                He will of course wish to thank you...

BARON: I do not need thanks at all Monsignor.

VALENCE: But it is such a generous gift, and in any
                case...

BARON: Thank you so much Monsignor.

[*He shoos the priest out. VALENCE exits. SFX intercom.*]

INGRID: The office again sir.

BARON: Fine.

SCHMIDT: Herr Baron I have the reconciliation,
                           everything taken into account.

BARON: I have just signed a cheque for a thousand
                           Crowns.

SCHMIDT: Very good sir. Then the positive balance
                           sent to the Ministry will be 297.000
                           Crowns. A very tidy sum to send in.

BARON: Thank you Schmidt. Have the return sent
                           round to the Ministry by messenger.

SCHMIDT: Yes sir, thank you.

[*Puts down telephone very deliberately.*]

BARON: 297 000 Crowns... A very tidy sum to send
                           in. Exactly as the Devil said. Word for
                           word. But he can't be the Devil. He does
                           not exist.

[*Pause. SFX intercom.*]

INGRID: His Eminence the Cardinal Archbishop is
                           here Herr Baron.

BARON: Please show him in.

[*BARON goes rapidly to greet the CARDINAL. He is a very impressive
figure, coming directly from saying Mass. Monsignor VALENCE is in
attendance.*]

CARDINAL: My dear Baron - your gift to my fund is so generous I must come to thank you in person.

BARON: Your Eminence does me too much honour.

CARDINAL: No. I take account not only of the financial amount but also of the spirit which led you to make such a gift.

BARON: I do no more than acknowledge your Eminence's wise and splendid initiatives.

CARDINAL: In any case Baron, I can only say that you have a special place in my heart. And you will I hope allow me to bless you.

[*BARON goes down on one knee. The CARDINAL blesses BARON.*]

CARDINAL: And now good morning Baron and all my continuing blessings.

BARON: Good morning Your Eminence.

[*BARON shows the CARDINAL out. He sits down suddenly on the same chair as the THE DEVIL sat on.*]

BARON: Something about all this must be true. Or anyway different to what I have always thought.

[*Pause.*]

                       If there's a Devil there must be a God... I'll go to the twelve o'clock Mass.

[*He speaks into the intercom.*]

Ingrid, I am going out for a meeting, and also lunch. If the market reports come in put them on my desk.

INGRID: Very good sir.

[*BARON exits. Pause. THE DEVIL enters and places a red envelope on the desk, looks around and leaves. Blackout.*]

END OF ACT 1

*Monsignor
palence*

ACT 2

[*The same scene, early afternoon. BARON enters.*]

BARON: [*Speaks into the intercom.*] Good afternoon
                    Ingrid.

INGRID: Good afternoon Herr Baron.

BARON: There's a red envelope on my desk. Where
                    did that come from?

INGRID: I do not know sir. It was there on your desk
                    when I brought in the market reports.

BARON: Just before twelve?

INGRID: Yes.

BARON: Anything else?

INGRID: Herr Schultmann has phoned twice sir. He
                    seems excited about something.

BARON: Very well. I had better speak to him.

[*BARON takes a page from the envelope.*]

                    [*Reads.*] "And you old boy are now the
                    leading atheist in Vienna."

                    I don't think I can stand much more of
                    this.

[*SFX intercom.*]

INGRID: Herr Schultmann on the telephone sir.

BARON: [*Speaks into the telephone.*] Bretzenny.

SCHULTMANN: Listen old boy the most sensational thing happened at the Club today. I got there about one and was cornered by Grossmann...

BARON: About his wretched pavilion I suppose.

SCHULTMANN: No. He said that this morning he had a visit from a madman who said he was the Devil.

[*BARON stiffens.*]

                 Hello! Are you there?

BARON: Yes... just waiting. Go on!

SCHULTMANN: Well how this guy got in and out no one knows as the servants saw no one.

BARON: Well if he was the Devil no one would see him.

SCHULTMANN: Oh really old boy... Anyway you know Grossmann, always abrupt. He just threw the man out.

BARON: So the purpose of the visit was not discovered?

SCHULTMANN: Oh yes. Apparently the so-called Devil asked for Grossmann's soul. Of course that set Grossman off on one of his lectures on the non-existence of God so how could there be a soul? But the Devil just about managed to get a word in to the effect that in exchange he would give Grossman good health.

BARON: Good health? That's ridiculous. Grossmann is one of the fittest men in Vienna. Have you seen him with a sabre? And he rides every day in the Prater.[2]

SCHULTMANN: So I asked Grossmann what he intended to do and he said he would order a large drink and toast the Devil, and then forget all about it.

BARON: And then he got on to his pavilion I suppose.

SCHULTMANN: Dear boy, he took two steps towards the bell to order a drink and dropped down dead!

BARON: Dead?!

SCHULTMANN: Yes. We ordered an ambulance but old Doctor Hedwig who was there said that he was clearly dead of a massive heart attack.

BARON: So maybe he should have dealt with the Devil?

SCHULTMANN: Oh come on... these things are just coincidences. Anyway that kills the pavilion idea, and you old boy are now the leading atheist in Vienna.

[BARON *lifts up the page from the red envelope and reads the same exact words.*]

                          Hello... are you there?

---

2 The Prater was the great park in Vienna, with both a funfair for the people and avenues to ride for the aristocracy and plutocracy. - DD

BARON: Yes sorry just looking at a message. Well maybe I am now the leading atheist but it's a bit unsettling.

SCHULTMANN: Don't tell me that you are starting to have doubts about your atheism?

BARON: Of course not. But the financial world is quite dramatic enough at the moment without this extra drama.

SCHULTMANN: OK old boy I'll see you later in the week.

BARON: Yes we can run over this Grossmann business then. Bye for now.

SCHULTMANN: Bye.

BARON: [*Aside.*] Yes I __AM__ having doubts about atheism. Who can I consult.? Go to the top. The Cardinal... I will confess the whole matter. [*Speaks into the intercom.*] Ingrid - can you get me the Cardinal's office.

[*Sits back.*]

At least Astrid need not worry any more about Grossmann revealing the facts about her son. Serve him right for acting like such a cad.

[*Pause. SFX intercom.*]

INGRID: The Cardinal's office on the telephone sir.. Monsignor Valence.

BARON: [*Speaks into the telephone.*] Bretzenny.

VALENCE: Oh good afternoon Baron. I am so pleased to hear from you after your splendid gift and as you know the Cardinal himself is delighted.

BARON: Monsignor this is very urgent. Can I have an appointment to see the Cardinal?

VALENCE: His Eminence just left for his retreat at the Monastery at Melk. He will be there until Thursday when he travels to Rome where he has an audience of the Holy Father.

BARON: When will he be back?

VALENCE: On Saturday. And I am sure that he would be pleased to see you... and...

BARON: Can you arrange for me to meet the Cardinal on Monday morning?

VALENCE: Of course Baron. I will get his office to confirm the time. And should he by chance be in touch with the office before then I will inform him of your wishes. May I add that...

BARON: I am very grateful Monsignor. Thank you so much.

[*BARON ends the call.*]

BARON: Well I don't suppose a few days will matter. I will go over the whole thing with Schultmann. I can't bottle all this up much longer.

[*SFX intercom.*]

INGRID: I have the Minister of Finance on the telephone sir.

BARON: Please put him through. [*Aside.*] A few hours ago I would have been horrified by such a call. [*Speaks into the telephone.*] Bretzenny.

EISENTHAL: [*The Count's voice is authoritative, the voice of a man sure of his grand position.*] Ah... good afternoon Baron.

BARON: Good afternoon Count.

EISENTHAL: Bretzenny, I want to ask you a favour. As you know I have a pretty good experience of the financial world but I am not especially knowledgeable about the details of banking operations.

As you can imagine in the present difficult situation that is a gap I need to fill and I wondered if you would agree to act as my advisor? This would be quite a heavy task I warn you.

BARON: My dear Count I am honoured by your suggestion but my bank is no more than medium sized and...

EISENTHAL: That is just why you could help. If I were to ask a representative of one of the large banks there would be too many complicated conflicts of interest.

BARON: I see... [*Pause.*] ...Of course I accept.

EISENTHAL: I have to add that the strength of your bank
                        as shown on today's return sets you apart
                        from most other banks in Vienna.

BARON: Sometimes fortune smiles on those who do
                        not deserve it.

EISENTHAL: You are too modest. But even if you had
                        the luck of the Devil...

[*BARON reacts as this comment hits him. Eisenthal continues in a lighter,
yet still detached, tone.*]

                        ...my decision would not change - I think
                        it was Napoleon who said that he would
                        prefer a lucky general to a clever one, and
                        no doubt the same applies to bankers.

BARON: Well, I cannot judge that. How do you
                        wish to proceed?

EISENTHAL: Let us lunch privately at the Ministry
                        tomorrow. Come at 12.30.

BARON: Very good. And I appreciate your
                        confidence.

EISENTHAL: Not at all. And if you agree I shall announce
                        it in the Bulletin in the morning.

BARON: Yes of course.

EISENTHAL: Till tomorrow then.

BARON: Till tomorrow.

[*Their phone call ends. Pause.*]

BARON: [*Speaks into the intercom.*] Ingrid please get me Herr Schultmann.

INGRID: Very good sir.

BARON: I must go over everything with Schultmann.

[*Pause. SFX intercom.*]

INGRID: I have Herr Schultmann, sir.

BARON: [*Speaks into the telephone.*] Bretzenny.

SCHULTMANN: Hi Hi old boy! Anything up?

BARON: Eisenthal, the Finance Minister, has just asked me to be his advisor.

SCHULTMANN: I hope you accepted.

BARON: Yes of course. It will be in the Bulletin in the morning.

SCHULTMANN: Is it true that Eisenthal looks at every banking return as soon as it comes in?

BARON: Yes. He had seen mine.

SCHULTMANN: Well done. You are a special man. That will show the chatterboxes in the market.

BARON: But I have had quite a day. Could we have a drink this evening. Not at the club - they will all be talking about Grossmann - come to my apartment.

SCHULTMANN: Yes... um. There is... um. [*Decides to report news he had thought to postpone.*] Oh well, I will tell you but it is rather confidential. You know I advise the Race Course?

BARON: Yes. I suppose they are a bit upset that they won't get Grossmann's pavilion.

SCHULTMANN: They've got it already. All the money has arrived in the account they set up for it. Yesterday they had a mere hundred and fifty Crowns and now the whole amount.

BARON: Who stumped up?

SCHULTMANN: Nobody knows. They can't trace the origin. They are in a bit of a flap because they don't want to accept the money if it comes from someone with a poor reputation...

BARON: [*Aside.*] I wonder what they'd think of the reputation of the Devil.

SCHULTMANN: ...That's why it's confidential for the moment.

BARON: Schultmann old man, I've been under pressure and I need your advice as well as that drink tonight. Come at 8 o'clock and don't be late.

SCHULTMANN: Right. I am absolutely at your disposal. I suggest fine cognac and then lots of champagne.

BARON: I had already decided on exactly that.

SCHULTMANN: We always think alike, old boy, especially on essential things like champagne.

BARON: Schultmann you are a real friend.

SCHULTMANN: Dear man I am always ready to help. Though the way things are going for your bank I wouldn't think there is much I need to do.

BARON: Well we will see this evening. Au revoir.

SCHULTMANN: Au revoir.

[*Their phone call ends. BARON leans back exhausted, rubbing his brow. Pause. THE DEVIL appears. BARON stays seated and waves him wearily to the chair.*]

BARON: I suppose you provided the cash for Grossmann's pavilion?

THE DEVIL: Yes. I was upset at your surprise when I acted as a gentleman in being discreet about my visit to Grossmann, so I thought I would do the gentlemanly thing as regards the pavilion.

BARON: Anyway your activities have exhausted me. I am going to have a drink with an old friend tonight and tell him everything.

THE DEVIL: Yes, with the Hine 1865.[3]

BARON: I am no longer surprised that you know everything.

---

3 1865 was one of the greatest years for cognac, and Hine is perhaps the most aristocratic of producers. You can, I think, get a bottle of the Hine 1865, should you wish to check for yourself, with a price, I would guess, at around £12,000. - DD

THE DEVIL: You believe in me now?

BARON: Yes... on alarmingly clear evidence. And as
                         there is a Devil I suppose there is a God.

THE DEVIL: I have every reason to report that there is,
                         especially as He is always interfering in my
                         activities.

BARON: I see. Well I certainly have had to revise my
                         view of the world. But... I hope that there
                         are no more dramas to come?

THE DEVIL: Well... um....

[*THE DEVIL looks embarrassed as though he has to venture on a delicate
topic.*]

                         The Cardinal blessed you this morning...

BARON: What about it?

THE DEVIL: We cannot access your soul. It is protected
                         by the blessing. It can't be done.

BARON: Didn't you foresee that?

THE DEVIL: Spiritual people like the Cardinal are
                         protected by a barrier. I can't get through
                         to them.

BARON: Well the deal is still in place.

THE DEVIL: Yes but I can't execute it...

[*THE DEVIL looks embarrassed. Pulls his gloves about etc.*]

BARON: Well what am I supposed to do about that?

THE DEVIL: We have to arrange for you to keep your
                      soul. Then the difficulty of taking it to Hell
                      will not arise.

BARON: I fear that the Crowns are already
                      committed.

THE DEVIL: I have another route.

BARON: And what is that?

THE DEVIL: The Pope is working on an Encyclical
                      saying that I do not exist. The title will be
                      Ad Deliramentum Expellendum. [*THE
                      DEVIL explodes in anger.*] TO EXPEL THE
                      DELUSION! ME! A DELUSION!!!

[*THE DEVIL rises.*]
                      A *RAVING* DELUSION!

BARON: How can the Church say that with so much
                      evil in the world?

THE DEVIL: He will argue that evil is not embodied in
                      the person of the Devil. [*Begins pacing in an
                      irritated manner.*] After all these years! ALL
                      THESE CENTURIES! It is lese majeste. ...
                      and it is your Cardinal that is urging him
                      to issue that Encyclical. It is his idea!

[*THE DEVIL sits. Begins to speak more quietly.*]

                      You stand well with him. You must
                      persuade him to drop the idea. You can
                      report to him today's events and so on...

BARON: And otherwise?

THE DEVIL: I shall take back the Crowns.

BARON: I would be bankrupted. This is blackmail.

THE DEVIL: Yes... I am rather good at that. In a polite
                    way of course.

BARON: The Cardinal is on retreat until he leaves
                    for Rome.

THE DEVIL: Yes but a member of his staff is a secret
                    atheist who is not therefore spiritually
                    protected. He has just heard about the
                    Encyclical. Hence I know too. And I also
                    know the Cardinal will return to his office
                    this afternoon for some hours, and your
                    message about a meeting with you will be
                    relayed to him.

BARON: Well I suppose that what I would have
                    to say to him on your behalf is not much
                    different from what I had planned to say to
                    him anyway.

THE DEVIL: Exactly. So you will proceed?

BARON: Yes. I cannot promise that I will be
                    successful.

[*THE DEVIL pauses in thought for a moment, then stands.*]

THE DEVIL: Well I cannot think of any other way to
                    stop this awful plan... And now you will
                    excuse me as I am rather upset. Imagine!
                    The faithful everywhere told that I am no
                    more than a figment of their imagination!
                    It is outrageous. Disgraceful.

[*THE DEVIL bows mechanically and exits in an irritated and preoccupied manner.*]

BARON: I really need that talk with Schultmann.

[*SFX intercom.*]

INGRID: Monsignor Valence on the line for you, sir.

BARON: Very good. [*Speaks into the telephone.*] Bretzenny.

VALENCE: Ah! Good afternoon Baron. His Eminence has returned unexpectedly for a few hours and can see you at the Cathedral at 6 o'clock if that would be suitable?

BARON: Admirable. Please thank his Eminence.

VALENCE: May I say that I am so pleased that His Eminence...

BARON: Thank you so much for arranging this Monsignor. Good afternoon.

[*Their telephone call ends. BARON speaks into the intercom.*]

                          Ingrid I shall be seeing the Cardinal this evening and will be leaving shortly.

INGRID: Very good sir. There is nothing outstanding.

BARON: Thank you. [*Aside.*] So I now have to see the Cardinal and then Schultmann. Well at least I will be able to offload this business a bit from my poor shoulders. Fancy! In one day to be appointed as advisor to the

Finance Minister and as advocate for the Devil.

[*He passes his hand across his brow. Exits. Blackout.*]

END OF ACT 2

The Cardinal Archbishop of Vienna

ACT 3

[The same scene. The next morning. BARON enters and speaks into the intercom.]

BARON: Good Morning Ingrid. Any calls this morning?

INGRID: Good Morning Herr Baron. Yes sir, Monsignor Valence, very early... He seemed agitated and anxious to speak with you and is waiting on the line.

BARON: Well put him through.

INGRID: The Monsignor, Herr Baron.

BARON: *[Speaks into the telephone.]* Bretzenny.

VALENCE: Baron, I am so anxious for your advice. Did you know that the Cardinal's visit to Rome was in order to develop an Encyclical?

BARON: Monsignor I...

VALENCE: He was assisting the Holy Father in the writing of the Encyclical and I was appointed to prepare the draft in Latin, for consideration by the Vatican. You can imagine...

BARON: Monsignor, these are not matters for me.

VALENCE: But Baron, his Eminence has now cancelled the whole plan. There will be no Encyclical. I am to work no longer on the draft. For me it is a tremendous loss...

BARON: You must ask His Eminence about that.

VALENCE: But could you not explain to me why...

BARON: Monsignor Valence, you cannot expect a
                        layman such as I am to advise on matters so
                        close to the Church and to His Eminence.
                        Please understand that.

VALENCE: Yes. You are right... I apologise, but I
                        could not think of anyone who might be
                        informed apart from yourself, as you saw
                        the Cardinal at length yesterday evening
                        when his change of mind seems to have
                        occurred.

BARON: There is the Cardinal himself. You should
                        consult him. He will no doubt explain
                        everything. Insofar as he can. Has he
                        resumed his retreat at Melk?

VALENCE: Yes.

BARON: Well when he returns and has a quiet
                        moment broach the matter.

VALENCE: Oh, yes Baron. That is wise advice. I am
                        very grateful.

BARON: So good morning.

[*BARON ends their telephone call.*]

                        Wow! Wow! Wow!

[*Rises and walks around happily.*]

BARON: [*Speaks into the intercom.*] Ingrid please get
                          me Herr Schultmann.

[*Pause. He is excited, walks up and down his office then sits on the chair for
visitors. SFX intercom.*]

INGRID: Herr Schultmann sir.

[*The following conversation is conducted energetically.*]

SCHULTMANN: Hello!

BARON: Hello!

SCHULTMANN: Have you found out what has happened?

BARON: Yes.

SCHULTMANN: From the Cardinal?

BARON: No from his staff. Quite by accident.

SCHULTMANN: And...?

BARON: The Cardinal has cancelled the idea of the
                          Encyclical.

SCHULTMANN: Wonderful! Well done! The Devil will be
                          pleased.

BARON: Schultmann - thank you for all your advice
                          last night.

SCHULTMANN: Dear boy, if anything I was a hindrance as
                          it took so long to persuade me you were
                          not completely mad. But as you went over
                          everything - well you could hardly have

                              made all that up! The story was just too
                              complicated to be fiction.

BARON: I could only relax when you believed me.

SCHULTMANN: The money for Grossmann's pavilion
                              really persuaded me. And maybe the Hine
                              helped – it is dramatically elegant, the
                              most perfect cognac.

BARON: Yes.... And unless His Infernal Majesty
                              has something else up his sleeve I can now
                              relax a bit further.

SCHULTMANN: And I will go off and see the people at the
                              Race Course... whilst of course pretending
                              that I have not the slightest idea where the
                              money for the pavilion came from!

BARON: Good. And again thanks.

SCHULTMANN: Bye for now.

[*Their telephone call ends. SFX intercom.*]

INGRID: Madame Bernhardi is here Herr Baron.

BARON: Oh good. Show her in.

[*Mme Bernhardi enters.*]

MME BERNHARDI: Baron. Why this change of plan?

BARON: You have heard that Grossmann is dead?

MME BERNHARDI: Yes. But after I heard I could not reach
                              you, and then I received your note about
                              calling on you here.

BARON:	And so my dear the danger has passed. Please sit down.

[*They sit.*]

MME BERNHARDI:	And I have grown up. I can see that my life was less than splendid.
BARON:	I have had a moment of reality also.....
MME BERNHARDI:	I am giving up my little list...
BARON:	Of lovers?
MME BERNHARDI:	Yes. Except for...
BARON:	Except for me?
MME BERNHARDI:	Yes Sergei. You know how it is with me. But I will have to withdraw Peter from Eton.
BARON:	You must let me cover the fees.
MME BERNHARDI:	I cannot ask you for so much.
BARON:	You could if you were my wife.

[*MME BERNHARDI is frozen by the tension of the moment. Then she stands. BARON goes to comfort her. They embrace and are silent for a moment.*]

BARON:	It is to my shame that I did not propose before.
MME BERNHARDI:	My happiness now renders the past irrelevant.

BARON:	My dear let us dine tonight. Chez moi. All alone and happy.
MME BERNHARDI:	So happy.

[*She dabs her eyes.*]

BARON:	Now I have to clear my desk. I am lunching with the Minister of Finance.
MME BERNHARDI:	At eight tonight?
BARON:	Yes. And use the other door so that you can leave without seeing Ingrid.

[*They embrace and MME BERNHARDI leaves without further words. BARON takes a bottle of Cognac from his desk and pours a small glass.*]

Well there is some Hine left... And I certainly need it.

[*THE DEVIL appears.*]

BARON:	Will you have a glass?
THE DEVIL:	He who drinks infernal nectar has no need of the Hine 1865. I have modified da Ponte.[4]
BARON:	I hope that does not mean that you are going to drag me down into Hell like *Don Giovanni*.

---

4 Lorenzo da Ponte wrote the libretto for Mozart's great opera *Don Giovanni* (according to some authorities, his masterpiece). In the last act Don Giovanni offers a supper to the ghost of the Commendatore, who refuses on the grounds that beings from the next world do not consume earthly food and drink. The ghost then drags Don Giovanni down to Hell. - DD

THE DEVIL: No. Your soul is in the clear. I am going to the races to celebrate your success with the Cardinal.

BARON: You can see the site of Grossmann's pavilion – or should I say your pavilion?

THE DEVIL: Ha! And I shall of course be very charming to all the ladies.

BARON: Any woman in the world, I am sure...

THE DEVIL: You do not realise it but you are quoting Bulgakov.... he will give a lot away in his book about the Master and Margarita. Fortunately, it will be regarded as fiction.

BARON: Well you will be glad to know that I do not intend to write a book.

THE DEVIL: You will probably write a play.

BARON: I hope that there is no further shock for me in this visit of yours?

THE DEVIL: I have come to repay you for such a brilliant effort with the Cardinal.

BARON: I thought that concluded our earlier deal.

THE DEVIL: Yes, but you showed such ability. The way you persuaded the Cardinal that you had received funds from what could only be a satanic source but that your soul was protected by his blessing was a stupendous effort.

BARON: I had to hide from him that I had sold my
                      soul in the first place. And to emphasise
                      that I was saved by his blessing was tactful I
                      think?

THE DEVIL: More than tactful. It showed an amazing
                      sleight of hand. I must say that if eventually
                      you do appear...

[*Waves downwards.*]

                      ...below, I shall recruit you to my Infernal
                      Court. But for the time being I must do
                      something else. I will reveal to you that
                      Madame Bernhardi's son is also your son.

BARON: Good heavens! How can that be? Or does
                      she know?

THE DEVIL: No but she was... always wide in her choice
                      and the child was very blond and English
                      looking, just like her preferred lover of
                      the time, at the British Embassy. So she
                      easily assumed it was his child. He is now a
                      Duke... his social connections enabled him
                      to arrange for Peter to enter Eton, even
                      though he felt no need to offer financial
                      support to a woman with so many lovers.

BARON: My mother was English and blonde.

THE DEVIL: Yes, and your mother's characteristics have
                      come through in the son.

BARON: I intend to marry Mme Bernhardi.

THE DEVIL: I am aware of that. The news I have given will I suppose be a suitable gift for her this evening.

BARON: But how can I prove the fact without ....

THE DEVIL: There is no need to bring me into it. You and the son have a very rare blood group. It is statistically impossible for you not to be related.

BARON: Well all this is thanks to you.

THE DEVIL: No. It is thanks to you that I am still recognised as myself and not as a psychological construct - imagine! And it is a pleasure to deal with such a rational human. You have no idea how foolish most members of your race are.

BARON: And what are your plans now, if I may ask?

THE DEVIL: When the racing is over I will be arranging the early steps towards the discovery of the atomic bomb. I am after all the Father of Evil.

BARON: Atomic...? What sort of bomb is that?

[*Blackout.*]

Acknowledgements

Huge thanks to the fabulous team at 49Knights - to Dan Lentell, Carys Boughton and John Tiratsoo for making the script not just an enjoyable read but also a good one.

...and finally, thanks for the tremendous support of the staff of the Garrick Club at the time of the first performance.

- David Damant

EDINBURGH49

REVIEWING BEYOND THE FRINGE

Welcome to *Edinburgh49*. Our team scours the
listings, checking out the best and the brightest
from Edinburgh's flourishing creative scene,
signposting the top places to score your arts fix.

Start with 52 weeks in the year, take away three,
and you have *Edinburgh49*. We provide year-round
reviews and arts stories from across Scotland's capital.
Edinburgh49 +3 is our dedicated summer festivals
coverage, giving us a chance to support friends old
and new with lively and insightful content.

Also published by 49Knights

SHAKESPEARE, HIS WIFE, AND THE DOG
by Philip Whitchurch
(ISBN 978-0-9931975-4-3)

April 1616 Shakespeare has returned to Stratford a rich famous and successful man but all's not well. Why is he so unhappy? Why can't he sleep? Why is his wife furious with him? Who is Will waiting for and why can't Anne find the dog? The secrets, lies, resentments and passions of a marriage laid bare. A sleepless night in Stratford, the one hour traffic of our play.

★ ★ ★ ★ ★

"A Bardian trainspotter's delight... this is a script which will belong to the ages" - *FringeReview*

"A joyous celebration of Language." - *The List*

★ ★ ★ ★ ★

PHILIP WHITCHURCH is an actor, director and writer. His film credits include *The English Patient, Blue Ice, Wondrous Oblivion* as well as *Beowulf and Grendel.*

Philip is well known to TV audiences as *The Bill's* Chief Inspector Philip Cato, Captain William Frederickson in *Sharpe,* and the neighbour, Tyler, in *My Hero.* From 1987 he narrated the children's television classic *The Shoe People.*

His West End credits include: The Inspector in *An Inspector Calls, The Changing Room, Ghost Stories* and the Dad in the musical *Billy Elliot,* a role he reprised on Broadway. Philip has also worked at the National Theatre, The Globe and the Royal Shakespeare Company.

Also published by 49Knights

A FISTFUL OF SPAGHETTI: THE SMASH HIT SPOOF WESTERN

by John Hewer
(ISBN 9780993197536)

Grab your guns, put on your spurs and laugh till you're O.K. Corral isn't O.K. anymore in this sure-fire send up of the Western genre!

When the simple townsfolk of Eagle-Creek-River-Hawk-River-Creek are jeopardised by the return of the evil One-Eyed Sid, the befuddled Mayor, the under-qualified Sheriff and the crazy Old Hag round up a posse, but it's no good; he isn't afraid of cats... As the death toll increases, there's only one man who can come to their rescue.... The legendary Drake Weston.

Let's just hope he ain't away on vacation...

Expect quick-fire puns, a whole bunch of good, bad and ugly characters and surreal slapstick in this all-out guns-blazin', thigh-slappin' poncho pastiche!

★ ★ ★ ★ ★

JOHN HEWER graduated from Northumbria University and holds a BA Hons. in Drama and Scriptwriting. He has also completed writing workshops at the Royal Court Theatre and Soho Theatre. John works as a freelance writer/director and runs annual scriptwriting workshops at the Riverhead Theatre, Louth.

RONNIE AND JONNY: FRIENDS DISUNITED

by Steve Griffin & Keith Muddiman
(ISBN 9780993197529)

Even at their peak, stand-up comedy duo Ronnie and Jonny were mediocre at best. But at least they were friends. When they had a dramatic falling out that led to a parting of ways five years ago, Jonny managed to make his way among Z-list celebrities while Ronnie became something of a recluse. Now they've been offered a chance to reunite for a high profile one-off gig – but can they shake off the past and work together again?

★ ★ ★ ★ ★

Ronnie & Jonny: Friends Disunited is written, and was first performed, by Steve Griffin and Keith Muddiman, who met at drama school. Griffin & Muddiman are an unlikely pairing of a well-spoken gent from the south of England and a big, straight-talking chap from the dodgy end of West Edinburgh. The pair bonded straight away over a shared loved of Britney Spears.

STEVE GRIFFIN is an actor, writer and theatre critic based in Edinburgh. *Ronnie and Jonny* marked both an Edinburgh Fringe debut and a comeback for Steve. 10 years earlier, in 2006, he produced the widely praised *Esme Tales*, while *Ronnie and Jonny* is his first outing as a playwright.

KEITH MUDDIMAN was the charismatic frontman of various bands on and off for 10 years before deciding to follow his love of acting. Prior to *Ronnie and Jonny* he had previously appeared in *The Overcoat* at the Edinburgh Fringe.

SOHO LIVES

by Mark Farrelly
(ISBN 9780993197512)

Two hit solo plays exploring the extraordinary lives and losses of two great Soho writers, Patrick Hamilton and Quentin Crisp. Greeted with huge acclaim since their debut productions, Mark Farrelly's plays offer actors and audiences laughter, heartbreak, and an urgent, passionate reminder that the only thing that ever matters is being true to yourself.

The Silence of Snow: The Life of Patrick Hamilton

"Magnetic" **** *The Times*
"Electric" **** *What's On Stage*

Quentin Crisp: Naked Hope

"Brilliant" **** *Time Out*
"Riveting" **** *British Theatre Guide*

★ ★ ★ ★ ★

MARK FARRELLY has been acting professionally since graduating from Jesus College, Cambridge. His West End credits include *Who's Afraid of Virginia Woolf?* opposite Matthew Kelly at Trafalgar Studios, and he has spent the last two years playing Patrick Hamilton and Quentin Crisp around the UK. He has also recently appeared in *Macbeth* at Germany's Globe Theatre, and written *Howerd's End*, a celebration of the upcoming centenary of Frankie Howerd, to be produced in 2016 and in which Mark will appear as the love of Frankie's life, Dennis Heymer.

POPE HEAD:
THE SECRET LIFE OF FRANCIS BACON

by Garry Roost

"So brilliant, it sent shivers down my spine." - *Malgosla Skawinski*, close friend of Francis Bacon

"Very, very unique and truthful." - *Clare Shenstone*, close friend of Francis Bacon

"A very good script, well researched." - *Eddie Gray*, close friend of Francis Bacon

Pope Head: The Secret Life of Francis Bacon is a solo show about the celebrated artist. He was an enigma, a maverick, a controversial & charismatic force of nature. This biographical script, written by English actor Garry Roost, will delight Bacon's fans old & new.

This critically acclaimed drama captures the life, psyche and sexuality of a troubled and troubling genius. Bacon's journey was a lifelong struggle with success and tragedy, a story which continues to inspire and intrigue in equal measure.

★ ★ ★ ★ ★

GARRY ROOST is an actor with extensive experience on TV, in theatre and film. His early career included the Theatre Royal Stratford East, The Citizens Theatre Glasgow, Birmingham Rep, West Yorkshire Playhouse and Hull Truck. Since 2008, he has played Alan Daniels in the BBC soap opera EastEnders. Garry is most often recognised in the street for his bit-part in Black Books – 'Creepy Guy Fiddling With His Balls at the Water Cooler' – a role which did not win him a BAFTA.